GARY HUME

Gary Hume was part of a celebrated group that studied at London's Goldsmiths College in the late 1980s. The public first saw his work in the near-legendary 1988 exhibition 'Freeze', organized by fellow student Damien Hirst. The door paintings that Hume displayed in 'Freeze' captured the attention of critics and collectors alike: over the space of a few months he went from being an unknown student to a sought-after young artist. Since then his imagery has developed, and he has come to be seen as one of the leading artists within a new generation of painters.

Hume was born in 1962 in Tenterden, Kent, south-east England. In the early 1980s he worked briefly in TV before deciding that he wanted to become an artist. He then spent two years attending Day Tech art classes at Chelsea School of Art before being accepted on the degree course at Liverpool Polytechnic in 1985. After a year at Liverpool, however, Hume transferred into the second year of the Goldsmiths degree course, and within a year of his 1988 graduation he had exhibited in New York and Germany and been the subject of a solo show at one of London's most influential new galleries.

By 1993 Hume had stopped making the door paintings and had developed a new pictorial style. In 1995 a solo exhibition of his work toured to several venues, including the ICA in London, and he was nominated for the Tate Gallery's Turner Prize the following year. Since then his work has been seen in solo exhibitions and important group exhibitions around the world, and been collected by major international museums. Hume won the Jerwood Painting Prize in 1997, represented Britain at the 1999 Venice Biennale, and in 2001 was elected a member of London's Royal Academy of Arts. He currently divides his time between his studios in London and upstate New York.

INTERVIEW

DAVID BARRETT **To understand your work it's useful to take a look at your painting technique – could you talk me through the process?**

GARY HUME Well, first of all I have to find an image. So it's trips to second-hand bookshops to buy material on whatever takes my fancy at the time – for instance, I've been buying lots of books on flowers recently. And then I sit down and trawl through those until I see a painting of mine.

An image that looks like it could be one of your paintings?

Yeah, I can tell straight away if I can use an image. I trace what I want of the image onto an acetate sheet with a marker pen. And then I put the drawing on a projector and project it onto the wall. Using the projector is a bit like doing photographic enlarging; you're zooming in and out with the scale all the time, rotating the drawing a bit, flipping it over, until you find the image that you're happy with. Then I'll measure where the drawing ends and order an aluminium panel to fit, or I may already have a panel that size. And although the drawing is only a part of the original image, I often end up cropping it a bit more when I'm projecting it. Usually I prefer the image to go off the edges of the panel – for it to be larger than the space I can capture it in.

And then you draw the image on the panel as it is projected?

Yeah, but with different tools depending on how each line will be treated: pencils if I'm not going to use the line – that is, if the two areas of colour are going to butt up against each other without a dividing line between them.

You've already decided whether colours will be separated by lines or not even before you mark the drawing on the panel?

Yes, that's right. If I plan to leave the line, I use a marker pen. If I plan to butt the paint up to itself I use pencil, and if I'm going to leave the line the base colour – or fill it in later – I draw on either side of the line.

When you get to applying the paint, are you working on the wall or the floor?

Almost always on the floor, and the paint is brushed, not – as some people think – poured. Well, every now and again I've poured an eye or something, but it's pretty much always brushed. There comes a point in each painting when I think it's finished, so I stand it up, and... it's such a disappointment. For some reason, having an oblique angle on the painting always makes it look better – partly because you know it's not finished – then as soon as you stand it up, it just says, 'You're telling me I'm finished but just look at how rubbish I am'. So then I might do some painting with it standing up, although it's more likely that I'll work out what to do, lay it down again and keep painting it. Initially there was very little repainting; I seemed to get what I wanted straight away. But as I know less and less about what I want there is more and more underpainting.

Are the colours chosen before you start projecting the drawing?

Yeah, the drawing normally tells me what colour it is. But then there's also a general palette of colours that I might be working in: a particular colour temperature for a body of work. And when you're working within a palette, you end up choosing drawings that will actually work in that palette. All the colours initially come from a chart, but I often just change the tone a little bit. For example, if I want to give a yellowness to everything, all the colours have to have a bit of yellow. Nowadays almost all the colours are adulterated.

And you use a white undercoat to define the details? Say the features of a face – they would be built up with raised layers of paint?

Not so much recently but, yes, in previous works like 'Patsy Kensit' [p.18] I would see the thick undercoat as make-up.

I would put the painting together like making-up a face: more eyeliner, more eyeshadow, a little bit of extra work on the cheeks, let's keep the nose small-looking, that sort of thing. That would all be done in white, and then the colour would go on top. But in the last year or so I've wanted the paintings to be very thin. So now they go straight from drawing to colour with no undercoat and any thickness change is due to me getting it wrong rather than any deliberate decision. But it was really just a very simple way of dealing with three-dimensional space on a two-dimensional surface. It's a very subtle perspective made up of layers of paint.

I've heard that you use insulating foam to define the areas to be painted.

That's to make an edge. In any of the paintings the edge is the only thing that matters. I used to think of the areas of colour as tectonic plates meeting, so in the paintings it's like there are these molten plates that would hit each other and dry. I wanted one of those plates to be higher than the other, and I wanted the hit to be more abrupt. I found that draught-excluder does the job perfectly, because you can cut it away after having puddled the paint into it.

You originally painted on canvas rather than aluminium panels – why did you change?

First off it no longer seemed conceptually important to work on canvas. For my initial door paintings I really felt it was necessary that they should be painted on a traditional painting support rather than something more door-like. But having done this for a period of time, I questioned how rigorous I needed to be [p.9] . Also, the smooth gloss surface – which was extremely laborious to achieve on canvas – proved to be terribly fragile.

Were you drawn to gloss paint because you were doing paintings of doors?

Initially yes: actual doors are painted with gloss paint so I should use it too. But only when I started using it did I realize how beautiful gloss paint is; the nature of it is so perfect. It's funny because I was doing painting and decorating at the time and got sacked for being too slow – when I was actually painting doors [laughs]. I said, 'I can't believe you're sacking me when I'm making paintings of doors in college as well!' But gloss paint has its own unique qualities; it's very different to oil paint, which can mimic different surfaces. For example, with an oil painting of a vase, you're aware the image is constructed out of paint but you feel that you know the material of the vase – you can tell that it is a clay vase. Whereas with gloss paint you are always aware that the picture is just a thin film of solidified liquid. And I like that as some sort of analogy of the way you think of an image, picturing it in your mind's eye: coloured liquids pooling against each other.

The door paintings brought you critical and commercial success straight from college.

Fortunately, the way I decided to paint them was very much in tune with the zeitgeist at the time: the tension between the image-as-an-object and the object-as-an-image, all that business. I was very lucky. The paintings wanted to be painted like that and they just so happened to fulfil the artistic and intellectual criteria of the moment.

Is it right that you asked other people to choose the colours for the door paintings?

Later on, yeah. There were other artists making colour abstracts, and I didn't want to be an abstract artist. Obviously my paintings had to have colours, but if I chose them I would end up investing them with an aesthetic – and that was never my purpose. Actually, I originally thought that I could just paint magnolia door paintings for the rest of my life, but I didn't have the tenacity to carry on indefinitely.

After the door paintings you experimented a lot, making sculptures and videos – like the video 'Me as King Cnut' [p.14]**.**

Well, 'Me as King Cnut' was to describe myself, the dilemma

that I was in. Was I deluded or was I all-powerful? It's a question you always have when you're creating things. Is this self-delusion, or is this an all-powerful creative freedom? It was a description of a perennial problem that, at the time, was incredibly pertinent.

And after all this experimentation, you returned to painting?

The sculptures that I made always fell down. I made a couple more videos but they were just tedious. So I knew that painting – or picture making – was the thing that I wanted to do. I felt like I might be good at that.

One of the first sets of paintings you made after the doors came out of your stay in Rome.

I was in Rome for a few months and was drawn to these ridiculously erotic, macho sculptures of athletes outside Mussolini's Olympic Stadium. I made some collages with silhouettes of these sculptures stuck onto gift-wrapping paper, and later made some paintings [p.20]. When it came to choosing the colours... for such a decorative painting it seemed right to take them from a packet of Wine Gums, where the colour signifies nothing other than personal preference.

No-one else was doing decorative paintings like that at the time, how did you feel about that?

It was nerve-racking. Decorative arts were treated with disdain in contemporary art at the time. But I was interested in the embarrassment, working within it. It seemed that without embarrassment I wouldn't move forward.

The style that you began to develop with the Rome works has informed all of your later pictures. One feature of this is the lack of foreground or background.

I really don't think of foregrounds and backgrounds at all – it's just a plane. If I think about a background then I've suddenly entered into a landscape, and I don't paint landscapes and I don't paint pictorial space. If I do choose a blue for a background then it might be a schematic for a particular kind of weather or a particular time of day, but I put no effort into making it recede because I have no purpose for doing that. It has to work on the plane for the painting to be successful.

So the colours function like colours on a map: declarative rather than naturalistic?

Yeah. I used to think of the paintings as topographies. There's no illusion of three-dimensional space in the works, but there is plenty of time: light time, because they change throughout the day. I never paint light, but I wanted to be able to have light in the pictures. And because the gloss reflects the light that we have – the sun and the artificial light – it can hold the light by reflecting it.

So they're not representations of other spaces, they are objects in themselves?

Well, that's what I try to do. They're not supposed to be allegories for anything. They're like you sat there, as far as I'm concerned.

You think of them as people?

The paintings have to define themselves because I'm incapable of defining them. The point at which they get rid of me and stand up for themselves, that's a hell of a relief – and they know it. I can't stand them at the moment. Being in my studio is like being at a bloody awful party [laughs].

Sounds like your studio is an emotional place...

I'm often in a rage with the paintings because they're unruly. But anger is a good emotion to have when painting; I have to kick myself into action sometimes because the pondering can go on and on, and you see too many options, none of which you're happy with. So in the end you have to get a bit rageful and just attack the painting and hope for the best. It's an emotionally busy time, painting.

There seems to be a definite cut-off point when each work is finished.

Well, they know when they're finished, and they say so. However there is a difficulty within that because really it's my choice when they're finished, and then the level of 'finished' becomes an issue. So I've got paintings that I have decided are finished, even though they still don't look finished. I know I could finish them off – complete them in the same way that I have completed other pictures – but by finishing them in that way they would no longer be questionable, no longer be new friends. Should I finish them off so that they become entirely believable—

—and just make the kinds of pictures you already know you can make?

Exactly, and become a production line. But you have doubts about changing, too; you think, 'Well, I like these finished-but-not-finished-as-I-know-I-could-finish-them paintings, but are they really interesting to anybody else, or are they just my little inquiry?' I'm in that stage at the moment; I don't know how to finish a painting these days because I'm a little bit bored of how I can finish a painting. I'd like to finish a painting in a different way, but it might mean that I'll end up having lots of terrible paintings – possibly – or really good paintings that are just different. It's a problem because you can become trapped in your own aesthetic. It's like when I stopped using shapes from magazine images: it got to the point where I could see the shape and already see the painting – the painting was already made in my head. And I don't want to make the paintings that I can already see; I want to make the paintings that I can't see.

This interview took place in October 2003 in a café near the artist's studio in Spitalfields, east London.

Additional interview material can be found at:
www.newartupclose.com

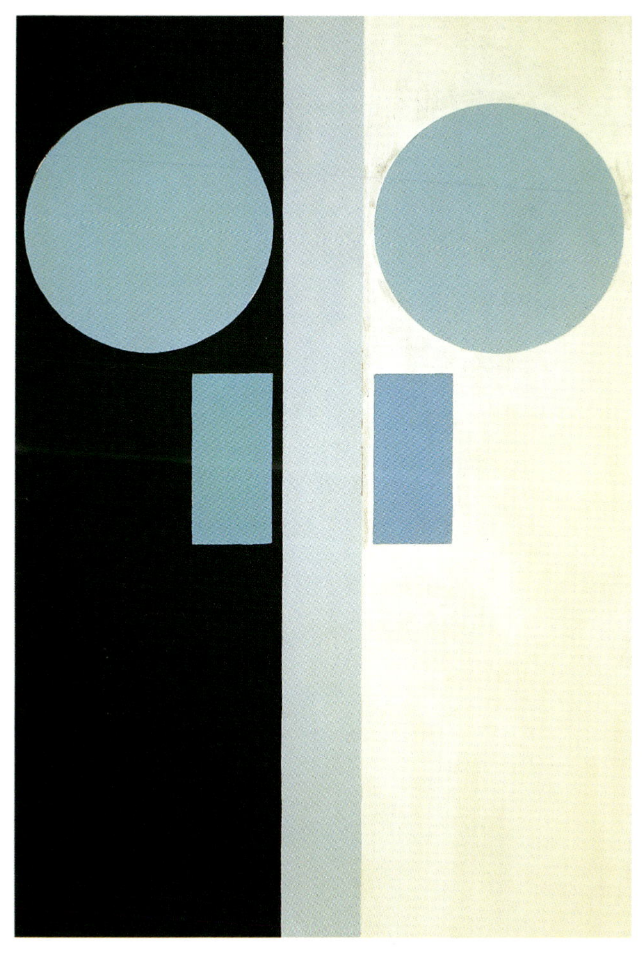

Dream

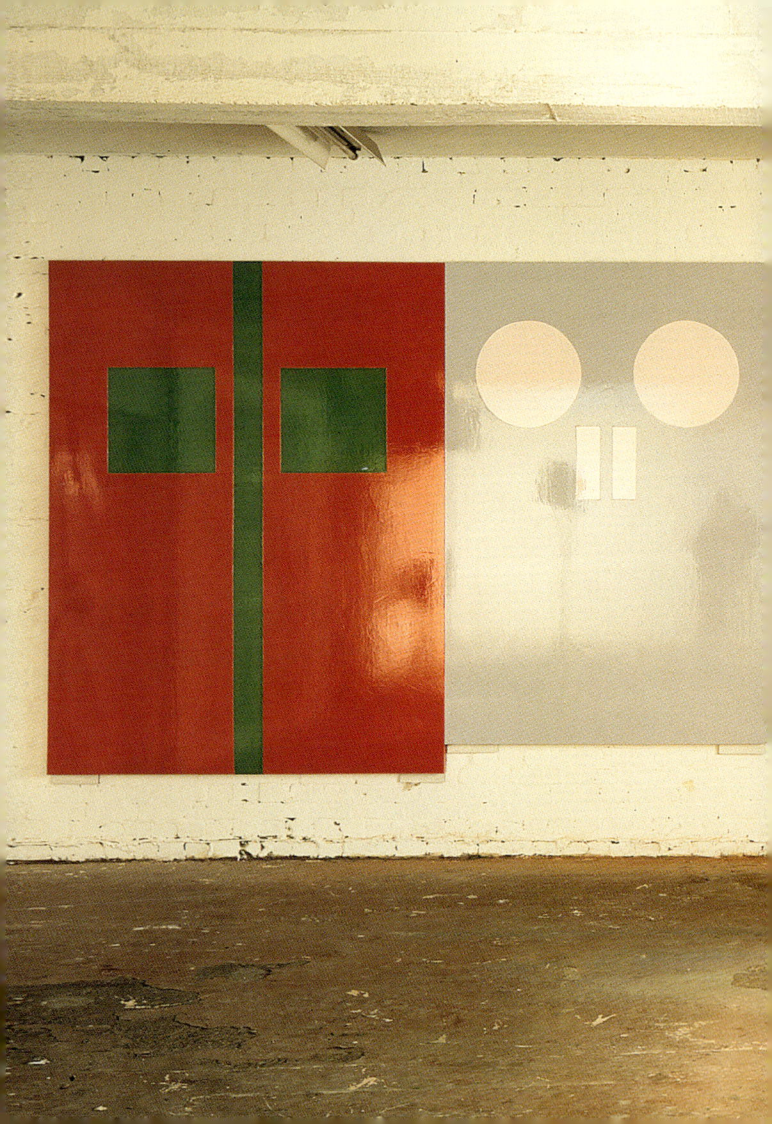

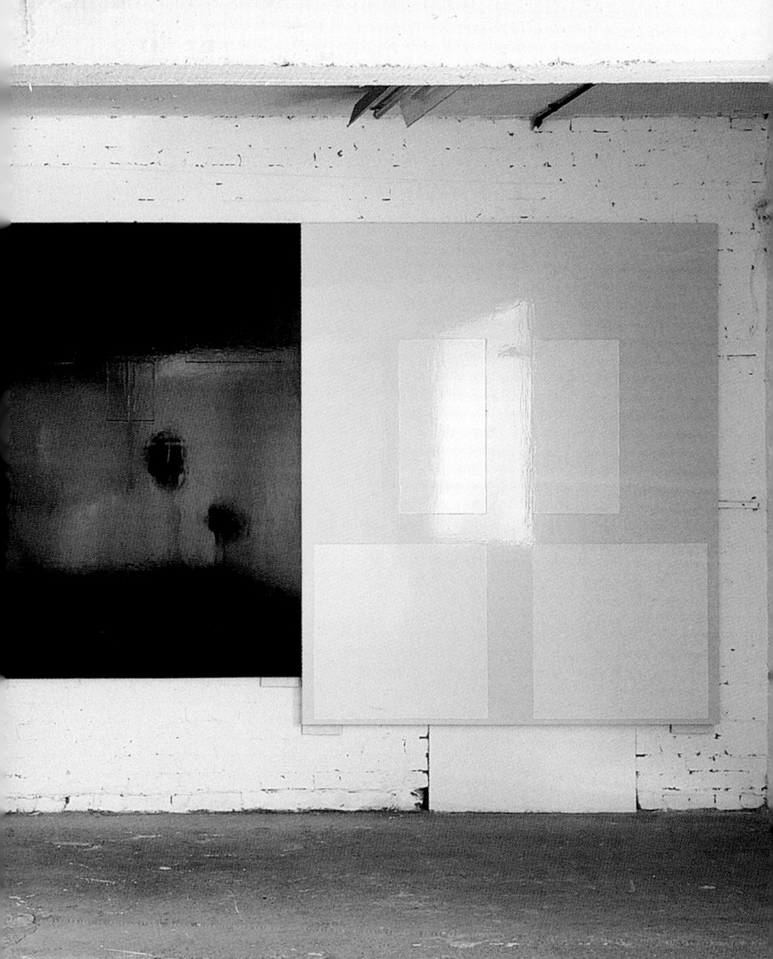

Dolphin Painting IV

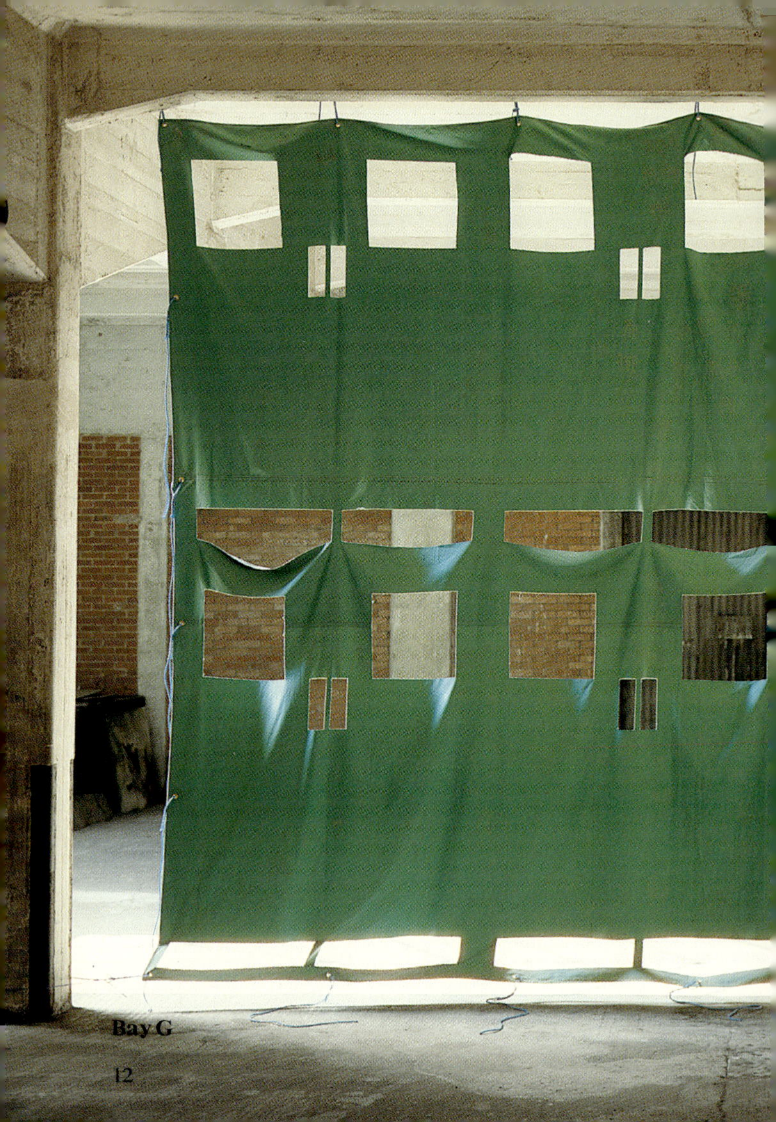

Bay G

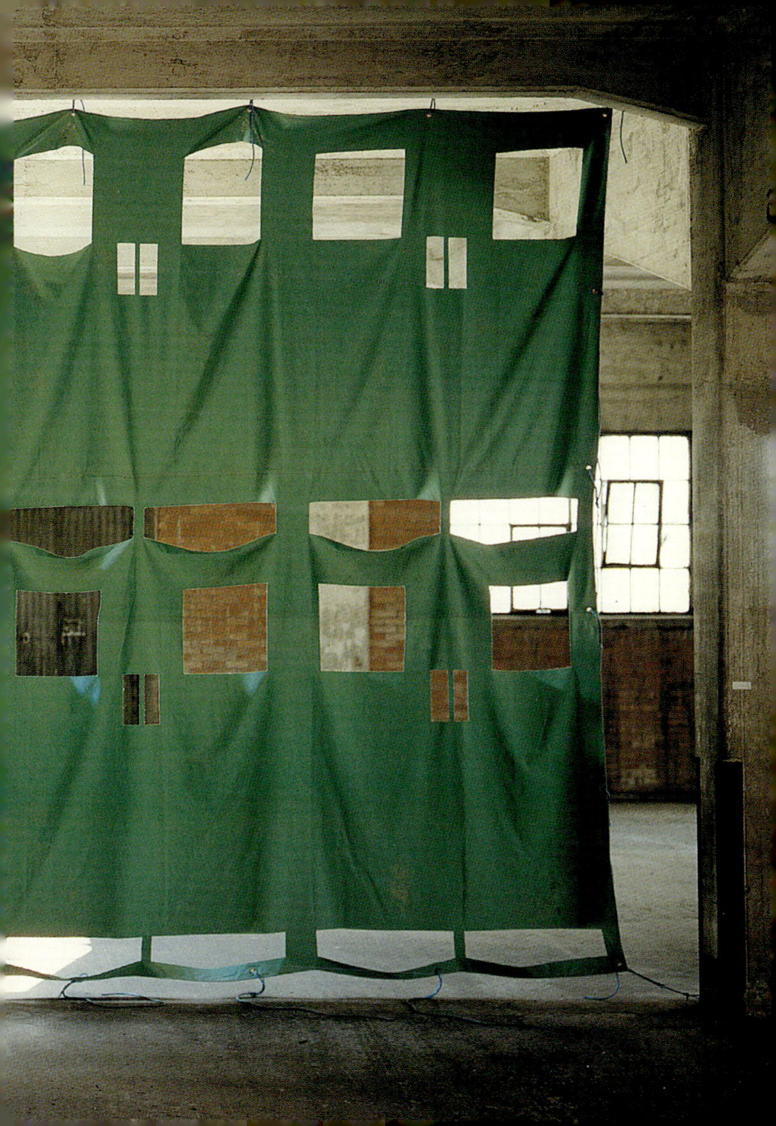

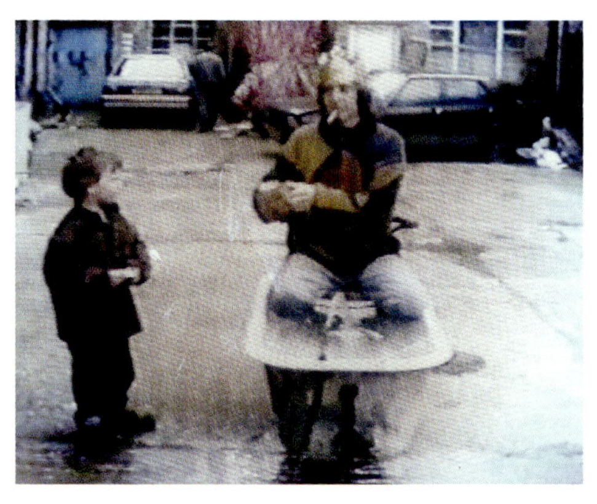

ABOVE **Me as King Cnut (video still)**
OPPOSITE **Tony Blackburn**

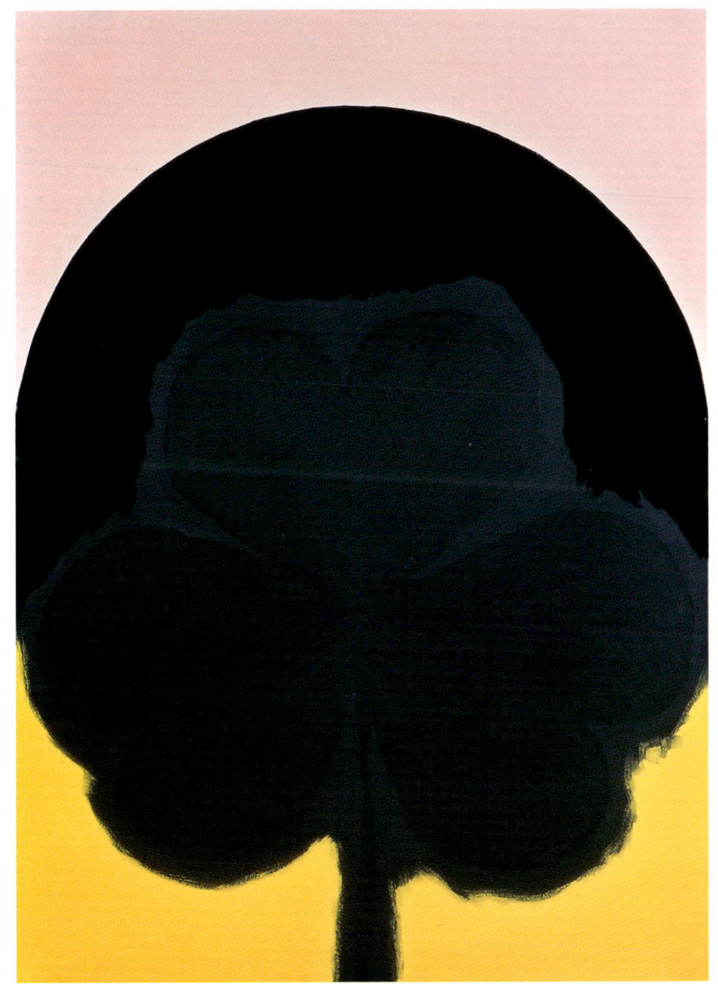

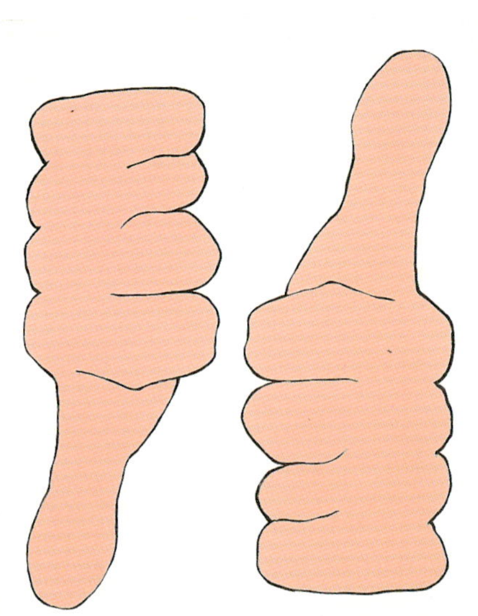

Hail Caesar

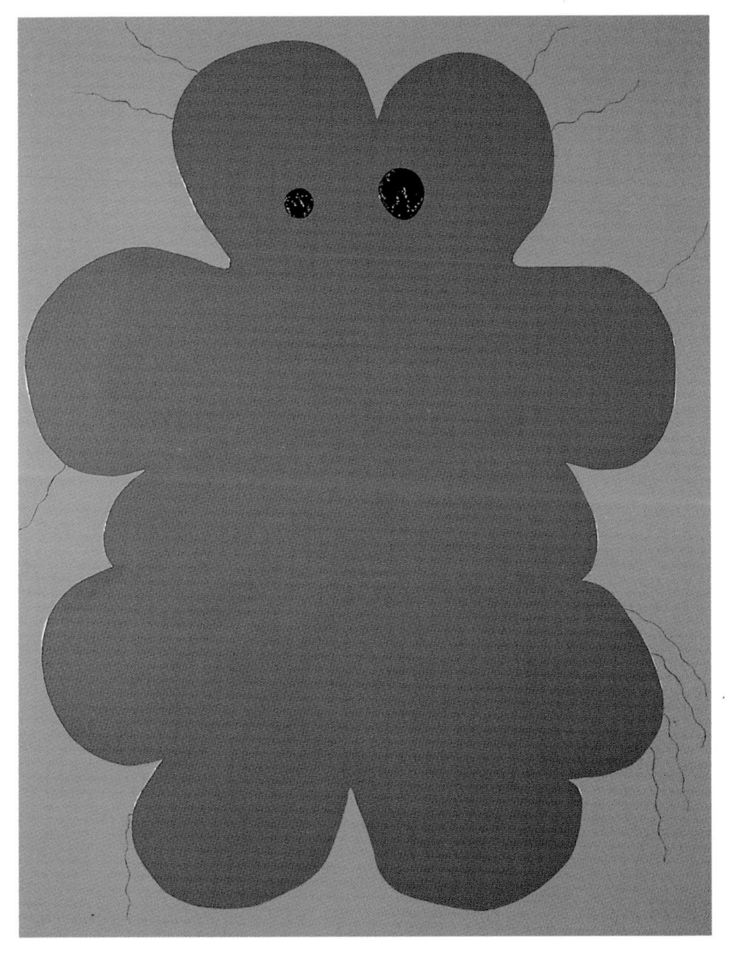

The Polar Bear

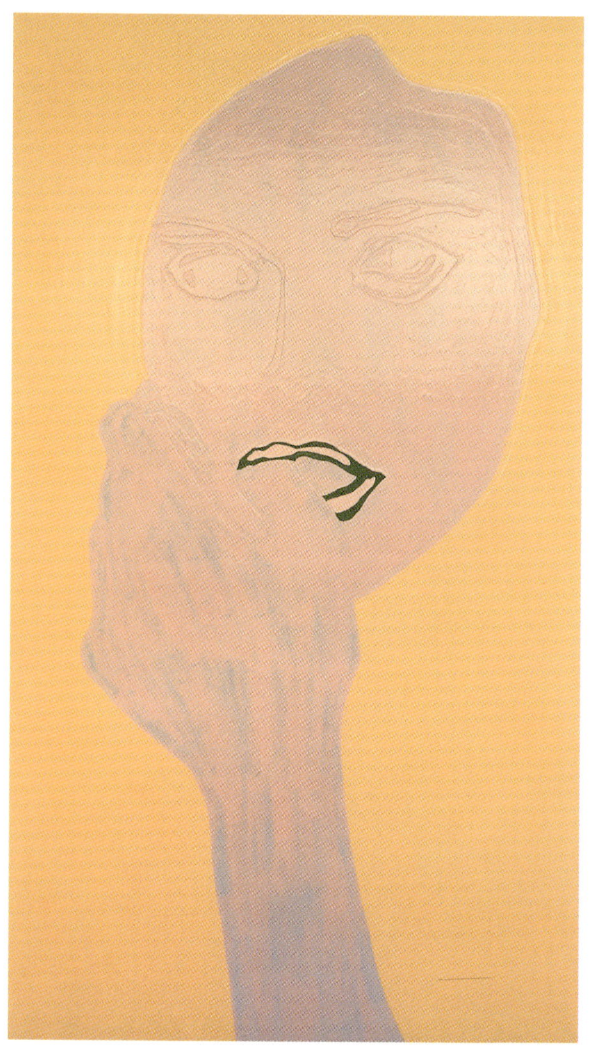

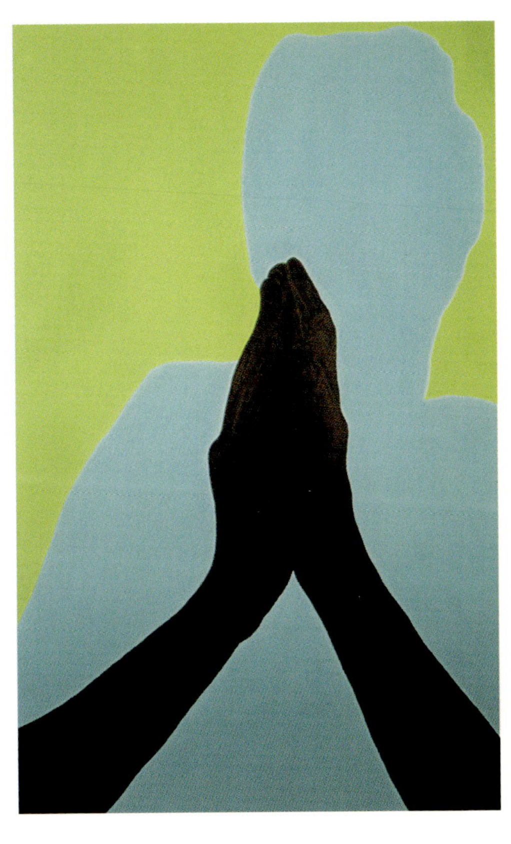

ABOVE **Begging For It**
OPPOSITE **Patsy Kensit**

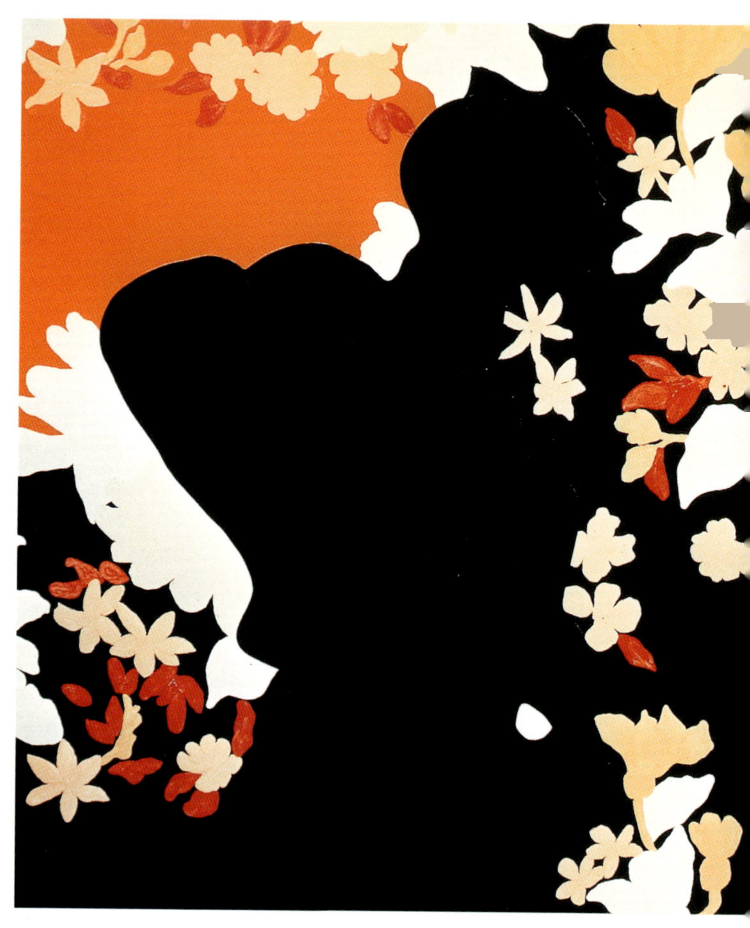

Love Love's Unlovable

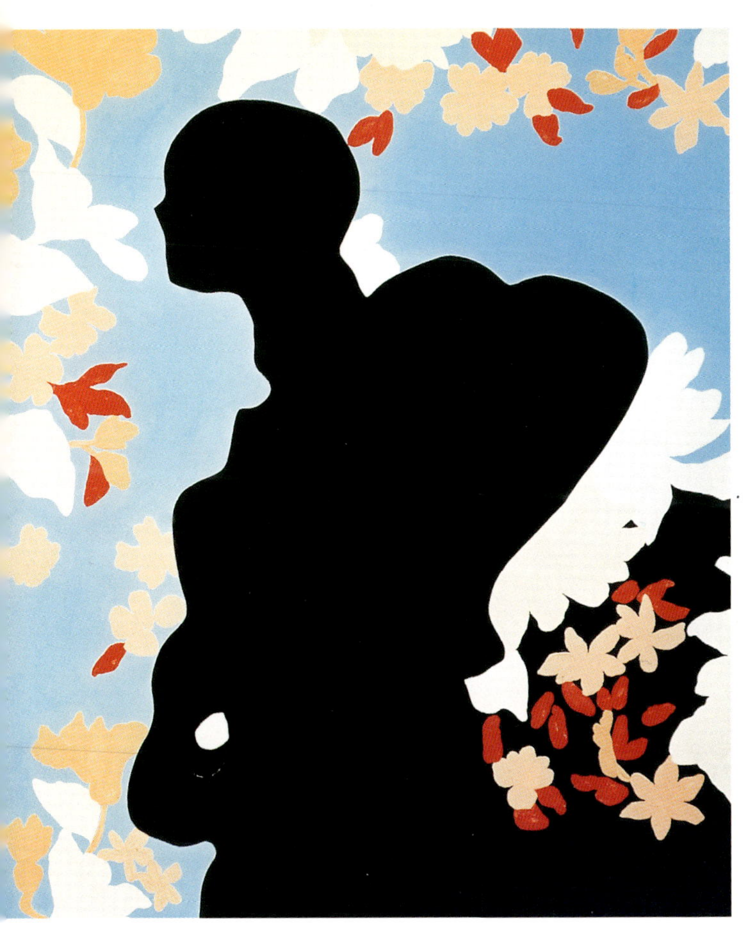

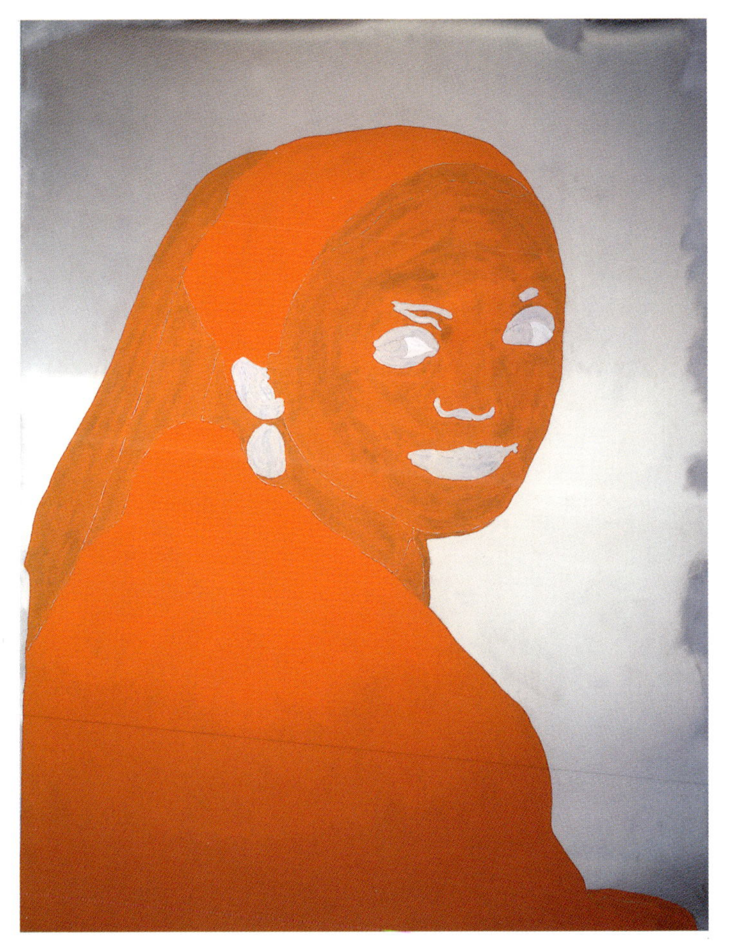

After Vermeer

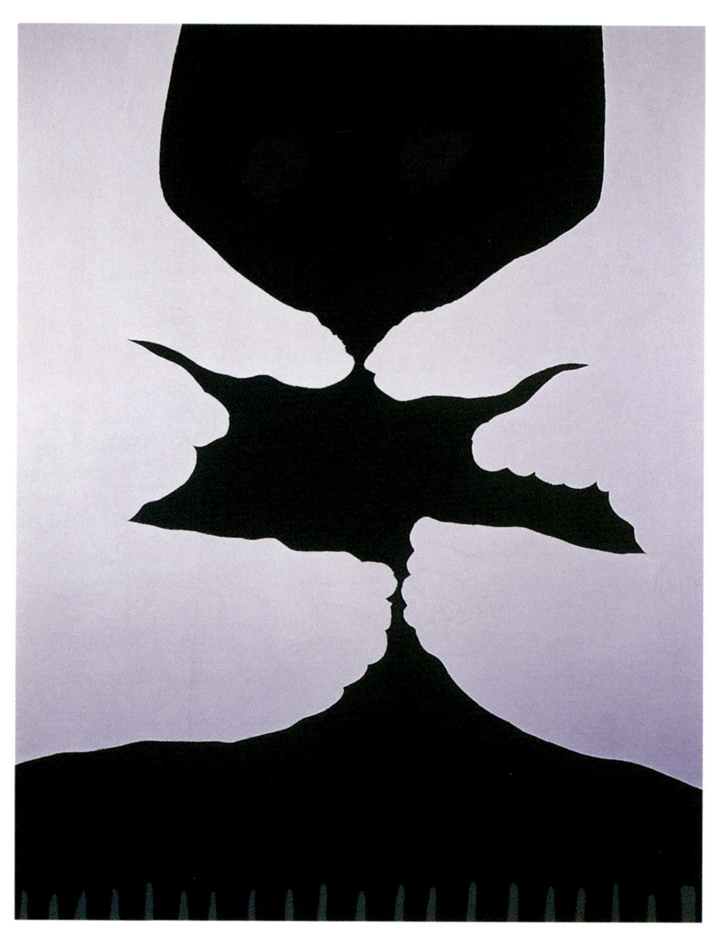

Four Feet in the Garden

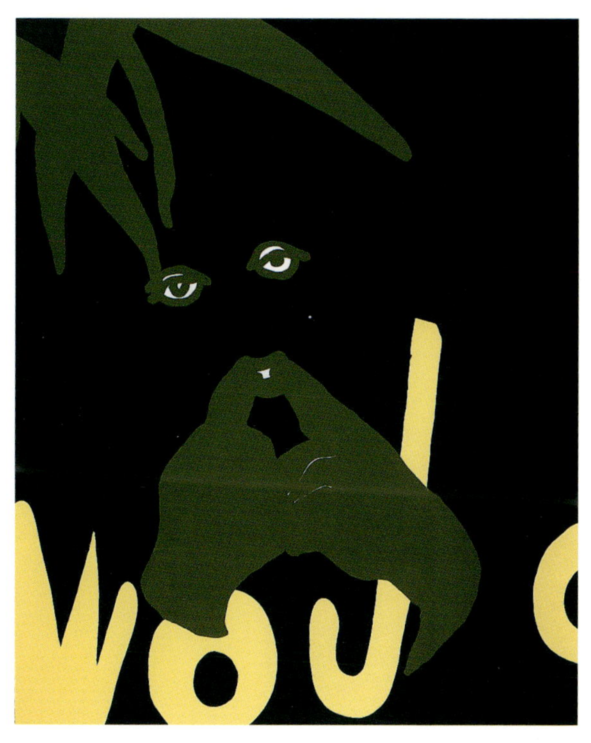

Whistler

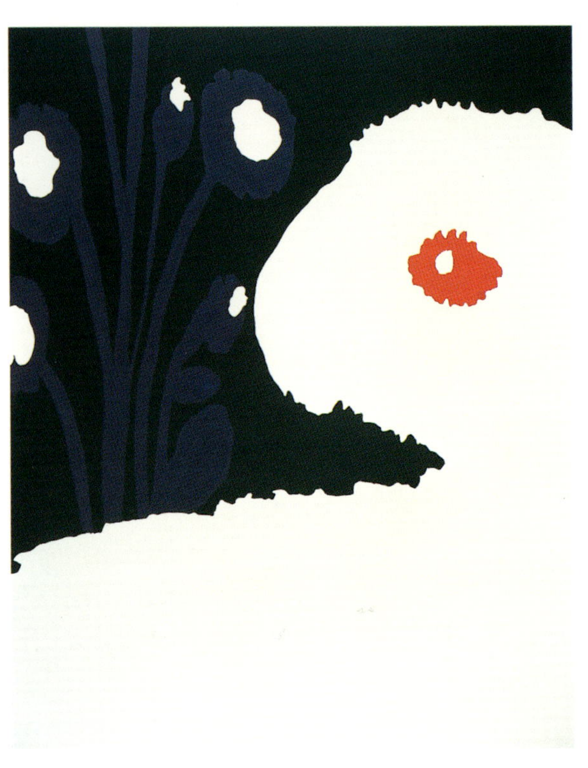

ABOVE **Garden Painting I**
OPPOSITE **Kate**

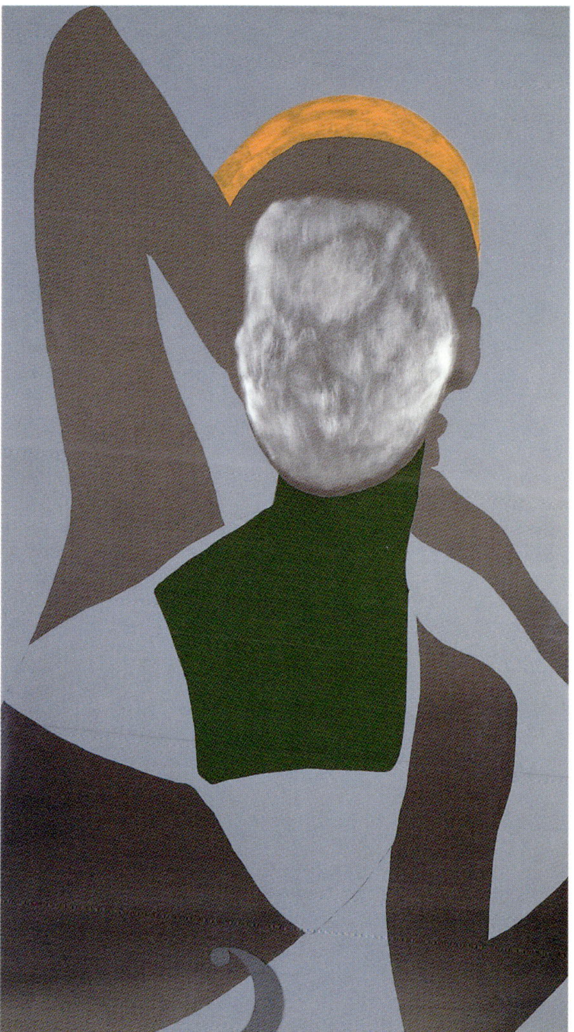

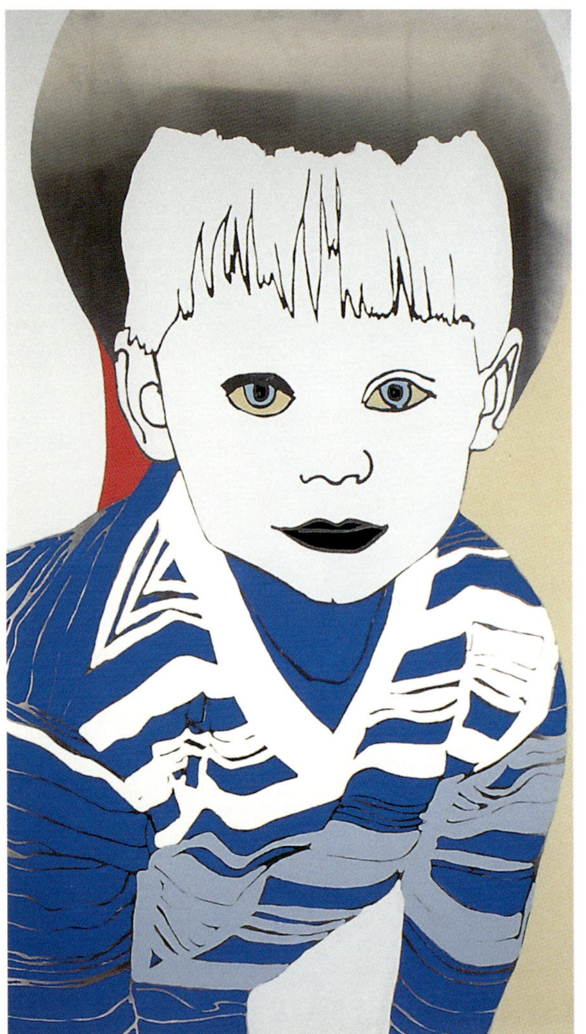

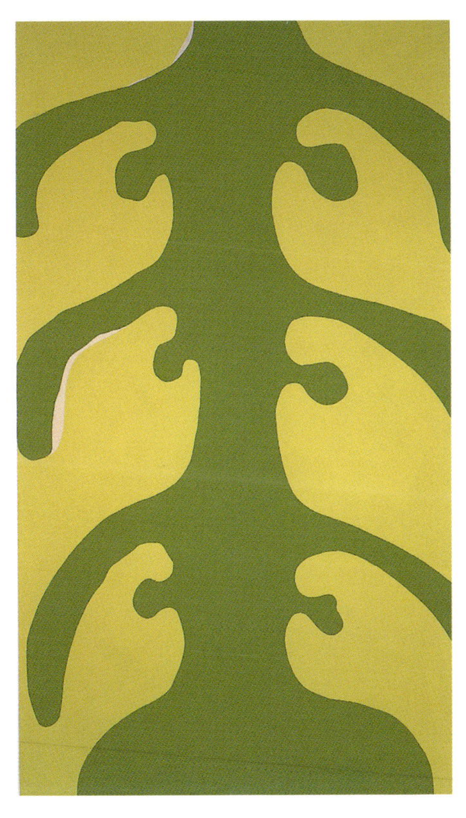

ABOVE **Birdsong**
OPPOSITE **Messiah**

Water Painting

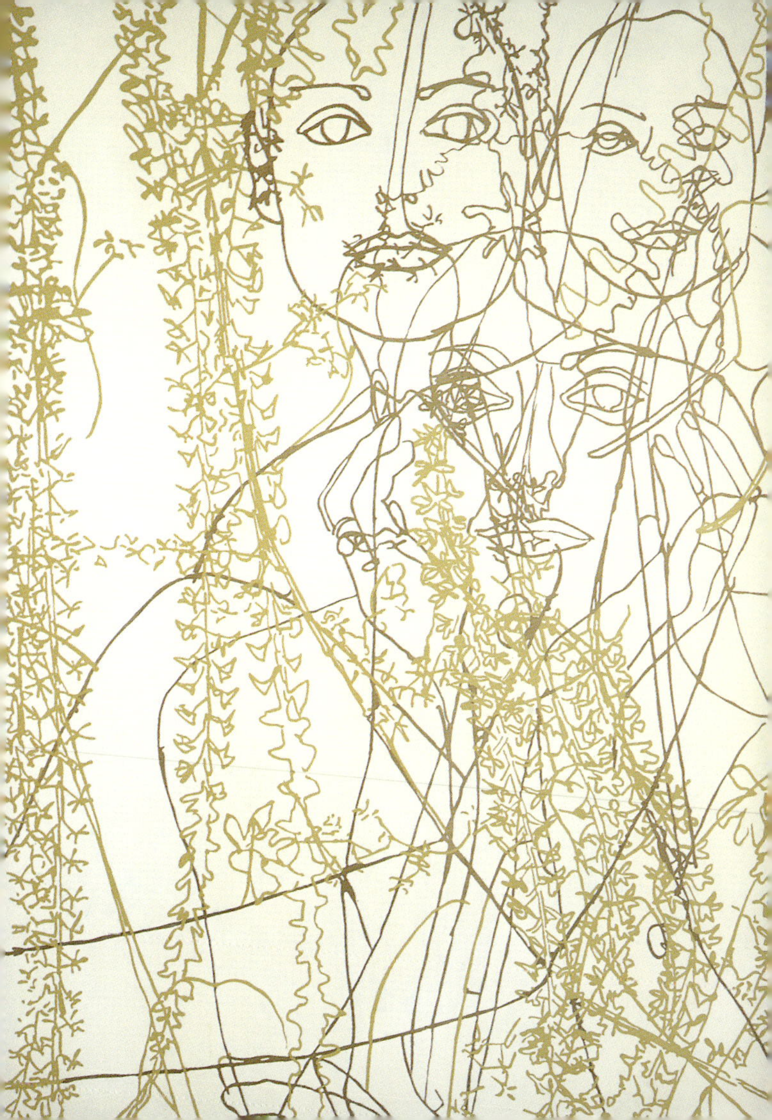

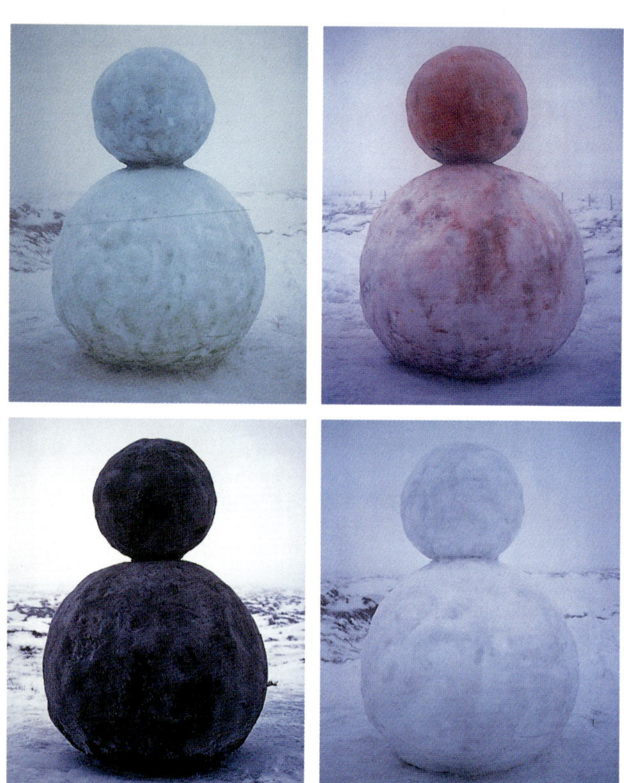

ABOVE **Snowman (×4)**
OPPOSITE **Snowman**

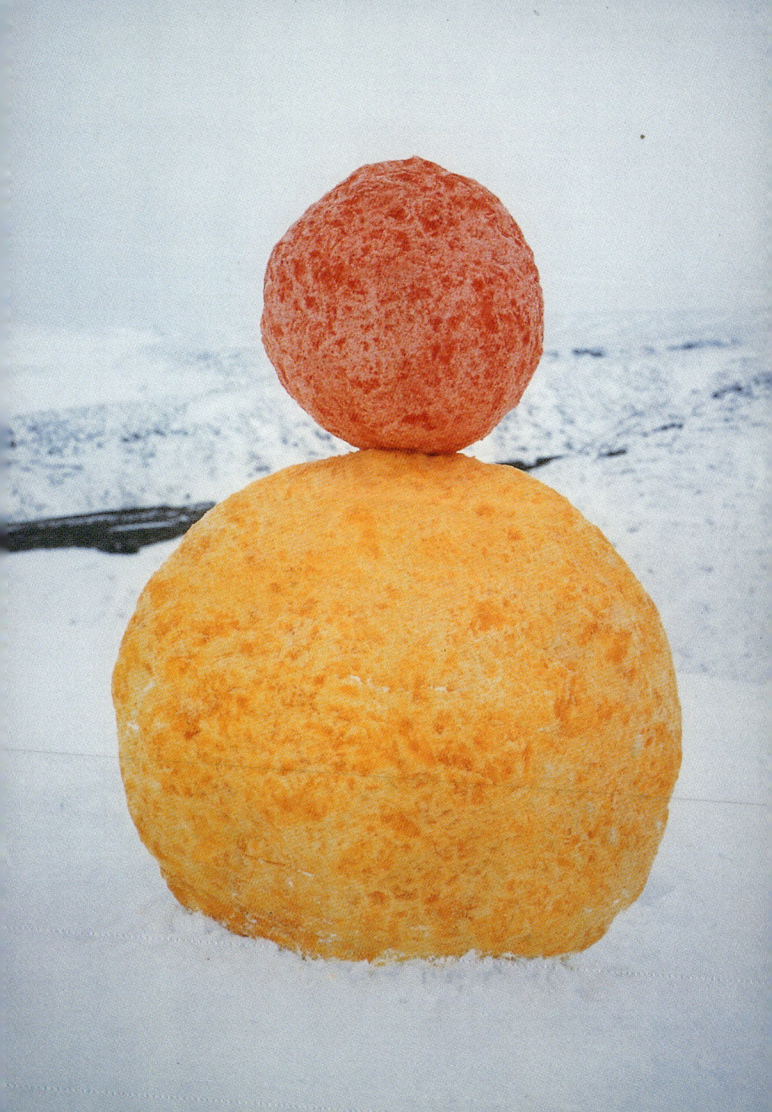

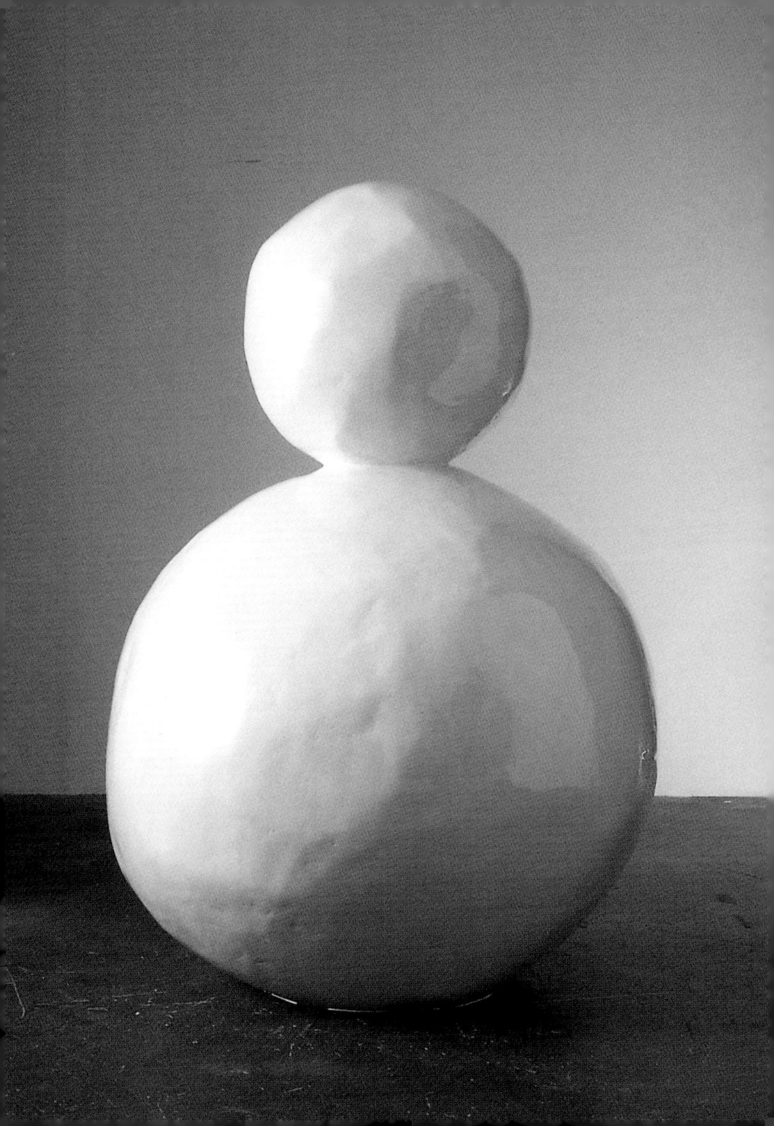

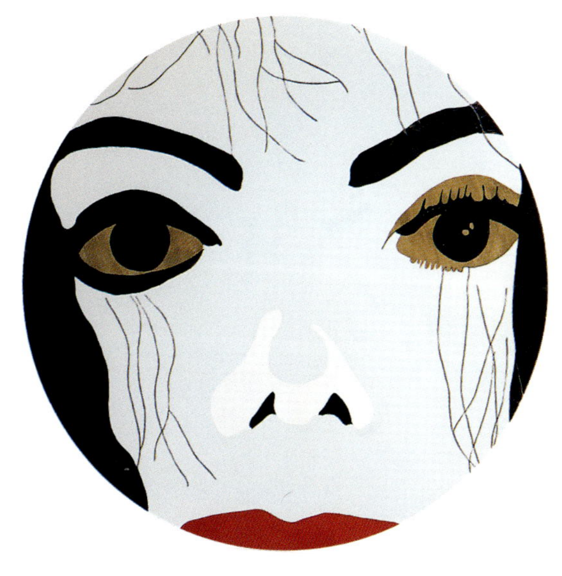

ABOVE **Michael**
OPPOSITE **Back of Snowman**

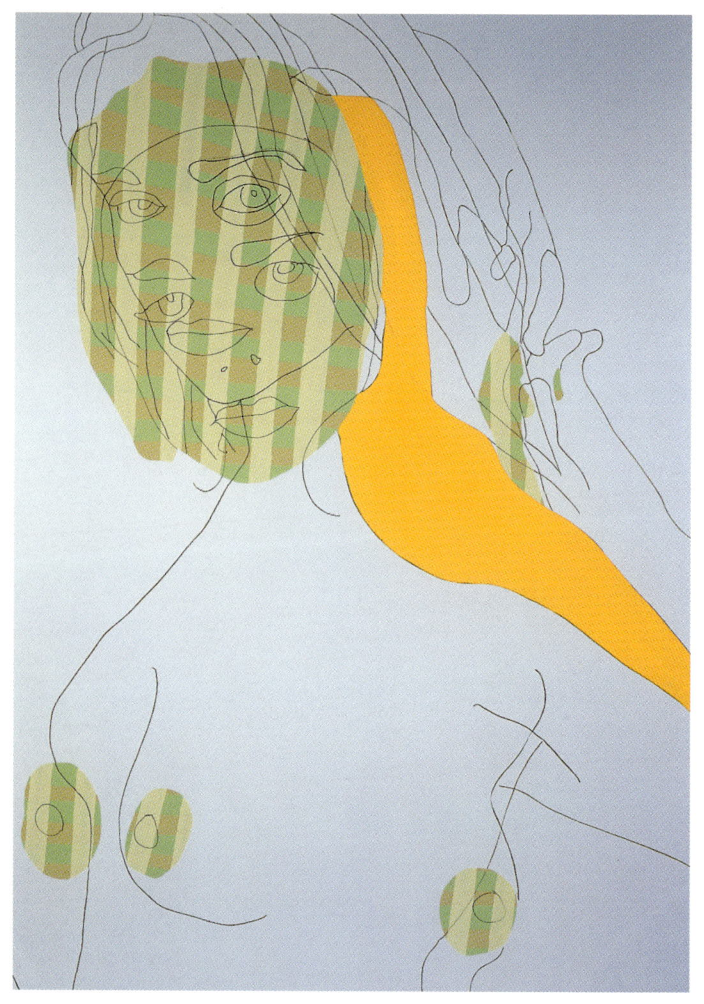

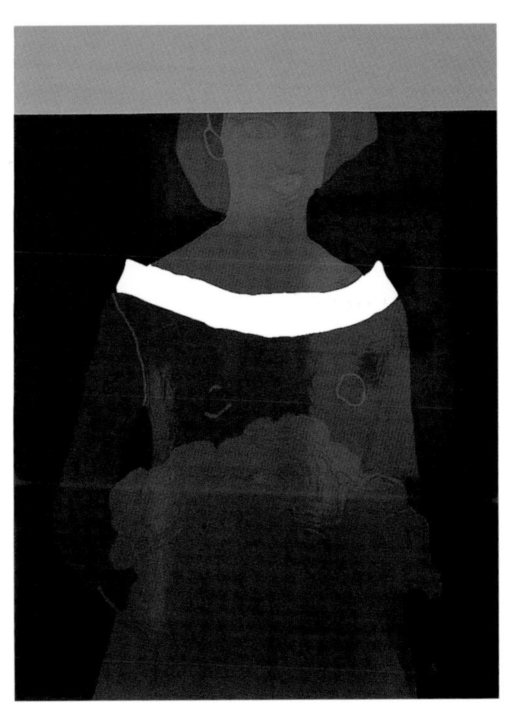

ABOVE **Green Hat**
OPPOSITE **Young Nun**

Dead Head

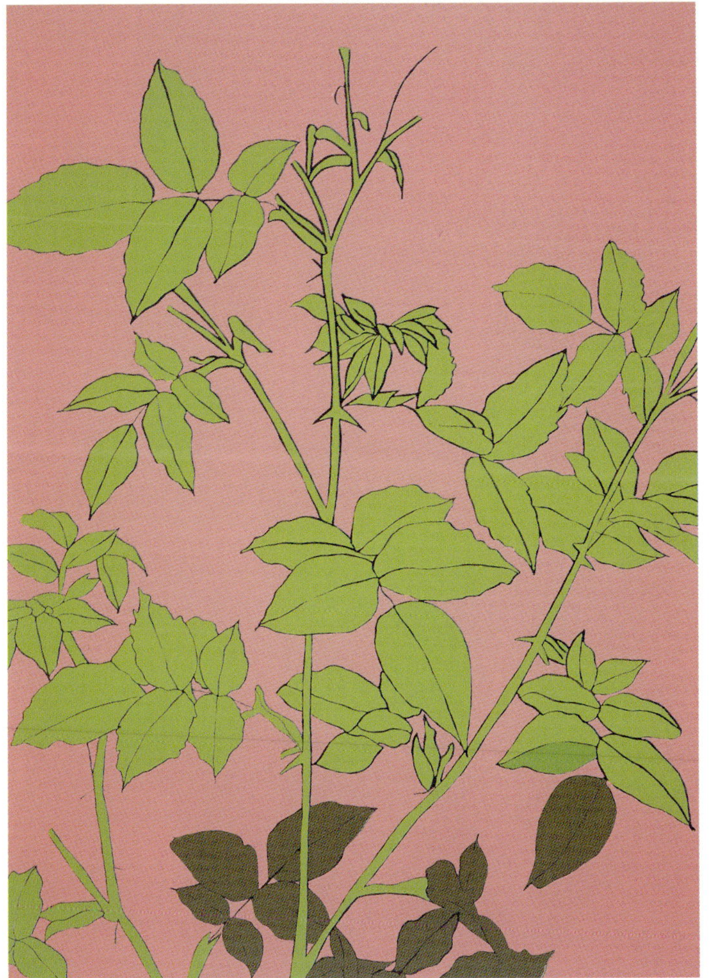

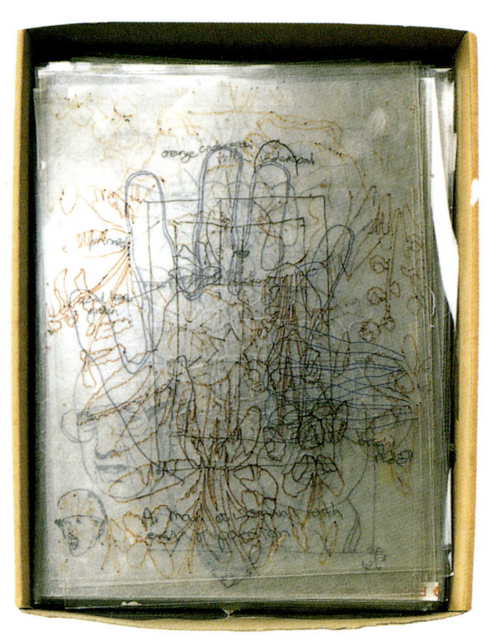

Box of acetate drawings

ARTWORK NOTES

9
Dream
1991
Gloss paint on panel
208 × 140 cm
'I didn't want them to have class references ... or design consciousness', Hume said of his door paintings, 'so I chose the kind of doors that we all go through at one time or another'. And those doors are hospital doors, in particular, the doors at Saint Bartholomew's Hospital, London. Hume would walk the hospital's corridors with a tape measure and notebook, measuring the doors, their porthole windows, push- and kick-plates. So, although the compositions themselves were entirely prosaic, the type of doors he depicted nevertheless had associations with life and death (on occasion, their symmetrical visages even resembled rudimentary skulls).

10
Dolphin Painting IV
1991
Gloss paint on MDF panel
222 × 643 cm
Hume's door paintings first brought him success when he exhibited early examples in 'Freeze', the celebrated warehouse exhibition organized by Damien Hirst in 1988. Critics hailed the fact that Hume's works could be seen as either representational paintings of doors, or just doors that had been painted. The artist's use of household gloss paint meant that the works hovered somewhere between abstract geometric painting (the 'Neo-Geo' movement of the late 1980s) and conceptual 'readymade' assemblages made up of everyday objects – in this case, doors. Hence Hume undercut the painterly pretensions of Neo-Geo abstraction with the pragmatics of the readymade, and found both camps enthusing about his work.

12
Bay G
1990
Tarpaulin
442 × 635 cm
The door imagery took on several forms over the years: from paintings on canvas to outdoor, billboard-style works; from wall paintings to hanging cut-outs. For the 'East Country Yard Show', a vast warehouse exhibition in south-east London, Hume produced large-scale tarpaulin hangings with repeated door motifs cut into the fabric.

14
Me as King Cnut
1993
Video
1 minute
The artist wears a cardboard crown from Burger King and sits

in an overflowing bath while his son, Joe, lights a cigarette for him. This video is based on the story of King Canute, King of England 1016-1035AD (Hume uses the archaic spelling, 'Cnut'). The legend tells of the king moving his court to a beach at low tide and commanding the waters not to rise. Of course they did, and the court nearly drowned. While some take this as a cautionary tale of self-delusion, others suggest that the king's intention was to prove to his obsequious followers that he was not all-powerful. Hume sees the two interpretations as analogous to the dilemma of artistic freedom.

15

Tony Blackburn

1993

Gloss and matt paint on panel

193 × 137 cm

Having decided to paint a lucky four-leaf clover, Hume set about searching the gardens of the council estate beside his studio for a specimen. Upon discovering only a three-leaf version he decided to treat his find as if it were four-leafed, concluding that you don't actually need great fortune to feel lucky. This portrait, of the cheesy British DJ Tony Blackburn, is one of Hume's most idiosyncratic uses of the plant. The appeal of Blackburn as a subject – with his jowly face and hemisphere of black hair – lay in the fact that he was considered a total loser. Having been the first voice on BBC Radio One when it launched in 1967, Blackburn left the station 17 years later after suffering a cringe-making, on-air emotional breakdown after his wife had left him. 'The veneer of everything being pappy and happy was gone', says Hume of this event, 'and suddenly here was the man'.

16

Hail Caesar

1993

Ink and acrylic on paper

152 × 122 cm

This work, with its thumbs-up and thumbs-down gestures, refers to the legendary tales of Roman Emperors deciding the fate of gladiators with just such hand signals. Hume often features hands in his paintings, and the thumbs-up motif itself has been seen in several works. 'Hail Caesar' has a partner work called 'Yes', which was produced in the same year and consists solely of a thumbs-up gesture. Another painting, 'Bear', of 1994, contains a thumbs-down image, but this time it is buried under the surface of the gloss paint and is only visible when the light catches it.

17 and front cover

The Polar Bear

1994

Gloss paint on aluminium

198 × 150 cm

Hume has made several bear paintings and prints using the same bulbous shape seen here. Each version employs its own set of colours, and some include additional elements: in the 1994 painting 'Bear' the creature is decorated with ribbons; while 'The Polar Bear', as seen here, sprouts wiggly black hairs. The generic bear shape itself has evolved from the artist's three-leaf clover motif and is made up of two overlapping clovers. The upper clover forms the bear's head, arms (or forelegs) and torso, while the lower clover only has two leaves visible, forming the hindlegs.

18
Patsy Kensit
1994
Gloss paint on MDF panel
208 × 117 cm
'I chose Patsy Kensit as a subject because she was useless, although she has regained her credibility since then', says Hume. 'It was a way of talking about the decorative painting style that I had adopted; it was a very English failure. The levels of stardom you can achieve in America and England are completely different, and there is a similar separation between the great American art and parochial English art. So to do a painting of Patsy Kensit was to say both that this is what our stars are like and this is what our painting is like, compared to the great and the good.'

19
Begging For It
1994
Gloss paint on MDF panel
200 × 150 cm
Hume was initially drawn to the figure in this work – which is taken from a magazine advertisement – because of the shapes that the hands made. His focus on the hands has led him to carefully delineate each finger with a raised layer of paint, while the rest of the figure is simply made up of flat pools of colour. Hume used the same image again the following year in a work entitled 'Falling', where the figure appears upside-down and the hands seem to be those of a diver in mid-air.

20
Love Love's Unlovable
1994
Gloss paint on aluminium
216 × 366 cm
Hume made several works inspired by the sculptures of athletes outside Mussolini's Olympic Stadium in Rome. First he collaged the statues' silhouettes onto flowered wrapping paper, and then he made paintings based on the results. Other works in this series include 'Vicious', whose colours are derived from a packet of Wine Gums; 'Hero', which is completely black; and 'Man, Woman, Jealousy and Passion', which features a woman's smile cut from a magazine and stuck on the end of a pencil so that it protrudes from the painting. 'Love Love's Unlovable' is the only piece in this group where the image is repeated symmetrically.

23
After Vermeer
1995
Gloss paint on aluminium
198 × 122 cm
This haunting work is based on the Dutch master Johannes Vermeer's painting, 'Study of a Young Woman', circa 1665-67, which hangs in New York's Metropolitan Museum of Art. Aside from rendering the figure in burning orange-red hues, Hume also flips the image so that the woman is facing to the right rather than the left, adding to the sense that you are seeing a negative image of the original. While the composition has been slightly cropped in Hume's work – giving it a longer, less square format – his painting is almost five times the height of Vermeer's tiny masterpiece.

24
Four Feet in the Garden
1995
Gloss paint on aluminium
221 × 172 cm
Hume is fond of making symmetrical paintings, and some even assume that he is deliberately referring to psychiatrists' Rorschach tests – although Hume himself denies this is his intention. He has spoken of this picture anecdotally as 'a suburban nightmare', and described a situation whereby couples might be enjoying the summer sun, wearing very little, when suddenly they find themselves in close proximity and an embarrassing sexual tension becomes apparent. Embarrassment is an emotion that Hume often draws upon as a motivation for making paintings: 'When I gave up irony, I took up embarrassment', he has said, 'and I prefer embarrassment'.

25
Whistler
1996
Gloss paint on aluminium
201 × 161 cm
Many people have taken the title of this image to refer to the 19th-century American artist, James Abbott McNeill Whistler, who was infamous in his day for championing the decorative in art, particularly with his dark 'Nocturne' paintings. While some may think Hume has similar intentions to Whistler, it is obvious that this painting does actually depict someone in the act of whistling – a loud, two-handed whistle at that. The odd yellow text at the bottom of the picture – which appears to read 'woic' – is simply the word 'blow' reversed and cropped.

26
Garden Painting I
1996
Gloss paint on aluminium
221 × 170 cm
Hume's 'Garden Paintings' are based on a group of 15th-century tapestries in the National Museum of the Middle Ages, Paris. Known as 'La Dame à la licorne', or 'The Lady with the unicorn', each

tapestry in the series represents a different sense. All of the tapestries, however, feature a central scene depicting a woman, a unicorn and a lion, surrounded by a backdrop teeming with plants and animals. It is from this background flora and fauna that Hume has taken his subjects – in this instance, a rabbit and flowers from the tapestry entitled 'La Vue', or 'Sight'.

27
Kate
1996
Gloss paint and paper on aluminium
209 × 117 cm
This depiction of supermodel Kate Moss uses an unusual technique: while most of the model's skin is left as bare, unpainted aluminium, for her face the metal has been burnished, presenting a scrubbed void where her features should appear. The orange halo suggests historical, religious paintings, a feeling reinforced by Hume: 'I wanted to do a Botticelli. I needed a Venus and Kate was perfect; being an image in a magazine means she's flat already and everybody knows her'. Hume has also made other works with the model; in 2000 he projected his line drawings of Moss onto her body for a series of photographs for British Vogue.

28
Messiah
1998
Gloss paint on aluminium
208 × 117 cm
Hume often bases paintings on his favourite historical artworks, doing so in a spirit of experimentation – curious to see what a contemporary version of a great master's work might look like. 'Messiah', although not based on a specific artwork, was inspired by the Byzantine religious icons the artist encountered while visiting the Ukrainian capital, Kiev. Hume's response was to produce a contemporary interpretation of this historical genre: 'I wanted to paint a picture of Jesus as a common little white boy, living in the estate round the corner'. In fact, the figure is based on a newspaper photograph.

29
Birdsong
1998
Gloss paint on aluminium
209 × 117 cm
'I wanted to make paintings of song', says Hume of his group of paintings that attempt to represent singing as a visual image. Often the pictures feature images of birds, or – as in this case – mention them in their titles. Generally these works are highly abstracted, and yet they retain figuratively familiar shapes. In 'Birdsong' the image suggests a spinal column and ribcage, as well as uvulas (the bit that hangs down at the back of the mouth) vibrating like they do in cartoons when a character shouts or sings loudly.

31

Water Painting

1999

Gloss paint on aluminium

305 × 242 cm

Although Hume's paintings start as line drawings, for years he was mainly concerned with the areas of colour rather than with the lines themselves. His 'Water Paintings', however, changed all that: 'One day I was looking at the pictures', says Hume, 'and instead of seeing the planes within the boundaries, I saw the lines. And it was a revelation to me; I thought, bloody hell, I've been doing this for years and I've never seen the lines', so he immediately began this new series. Hume overlaid several images in each painting because 'having seen the first line', he says, 'I then wanted another one'.

32, 33

Snowman (×5)

1997 [p.32]

2000 [p.33]

Colour photograph

158 × 122 cm

Hume and his old school friend, the artist Don Brown, visited the Peak District in the north of England to build a snowman that always looked away from the viewer, waiting for the thaw. Having made a white snowman, they then built more and coloured them with food dye. The 'Snowman' photographs are Hume's documentation of their efforts.

34

Back of Snowman

2001

Painted bronze

Height: 152 × Diameter: 125 cm

Hume's snowmen take several forms – paintings, prints, sculptures – and the shape has become as much of a signature emblem in his work as the door motif. 'The snowman is the perfect sculpture', Hume has said, 'like the door was the perfect painting. It works entirely in the round: you're supposed to be able to travel around it and there are no dead zones'. The sculptures are modelled in clay in Hume's studio before being cast in a foundry. The bronzes then return to the studio to be painted; 'It's always nice to have something in the studio that you can hug', he says.

35

Michael

2001

Gloss paint on aluminium

Diameter: 122 cm

'Well, I felt sorry for the poor blighter and just wanted to paint a sympathetic, tragic painting', says Hume of his decision to make a portrait of pop star Michael Jackson. Another factor in choosing this subject is that many of Hume's paintings are made up of diverse shapes that have been compositionally rearranged, which could be seen as similar to Jackson's surgical reworking of his own face. As Hume says, 'You make him out of composites, because that's what he is'.

36

Young Nun

2001

Gloss paint on aluminium

233 × 162 cm

This portrait was inspired by Paul Cézanne's 1896 painting, 'An Old Woman with a Rosary'. Hanging in London's National Gallery, it depicts a former nun who escaped from a convent and was taken on by the painter as a servant. Compared to the dark tones that envelop the French Impressionist's haunted figure, Hume's nun is painted with lively, exuberant colours. 'I just wanted to paint her as a woman who once wanted sex', says Hume, 'rather than a nun who forsook it and then lost her faith'. He also states that the stripes in the painting were to locate the figure at home: 'to domesticize her – give her a tablecloth, basically'.

37

Green Hat

2002

Gloss paint on aluminium

138 × 99 cm

This picture is based on a photograph from the Hume family album and shows the artist's mother acting as a bridesmaid. The 'hat' of the title is actually a green stripe across the top edge of the painting, far bigger than any normal hat. Hume describes the scale of the hat in this way: 'It was nice to make the hat big, not so that it was ridiculous – as in heaping ridicule on the figure – but just so that the figure is having to carry the hat, is sort of burdened by it'.

39

Dead Head

2003

Gloss paint on aluminium

95 × 68 cm

When asked about his subject matter, Hume once replied: 'I do flora, fauna and portraiture', but his disarmingly traditional response belies the oddness of his pictures. For example, in the paintings of flowers he produced during 2002-3, the whimsical imagery was subverted by such devices as removing the flower heads or darkening the palette to black on black. Omitting the painting's obvious focal point helped toward one of Hume's stated aims: 'If I can make a picture so it's like when you focus off into the distance, and you're thinking ... if the painting can be like that, I can bear looking at it'.

40

Box of acetate drawings

This is an example of a box from Hume's studio containing some of his acetate drawings: plastic sheets that he has traced images onto from books and magazines. These marker-pen drawings are used to project images onto the aluminium panels that he uses for his paintings. Hume rarely draws freehand – i.e. without tracing an image – as he dislikes the results, however he always has plenty of acetates to work from.

FURTHER READING

Jones, Jonathan, 'Gary Hume', The Irish Museum of Modern Art, Dublin, Ireland, 2003

Buck, Louisa, 'I want to abolish "me" in my art', The Art Newspaper, Sep, 2002

Cook, Angus, 'Gary Hume', White Cube, London, 2002

Clark, Candida, 'Doors of Perception', tate magazine, no.18, Summer, 1999

Hartley, Keith, 'Gary Hume', National Galleries of Scotland, UK, 1999

Batchelor, David, Adrian Searle, 'Gary Hume: XLVIII Venice Biennale', British Council, London, 1999

Bradley, Alexandra, Vicky Hayward, Robert Timms (eds.), 'Young British Art: The Saatchi Decade', Booth-Clibborn Editions, London, 1999

Buck, Louisa, 'Moving Targets: A User's Guide to British Art Now', Tate Gallery Publishing, London, 1997

Adams, Brooks, Lisa Jardine, Martin Maloney, Norman Rosenthal, Richard Shone, 'Sensation: Young British Artists from the Saatchi Collection', Royal Academy of Arts, London, 1997

Bovier, Lionel, Gregor Muir, Douglas Fogle, Parkett, no.48, Dec, 1996

Bonami, Francesco, 'Gary Hume', Bonnefantenmuseum, Maastricht, Netherlands, 1996

Bill, Simon, 'XXIII Bienal Internacional de São Paulo', Fundação Bienal de São Paulo, Brazil, 1996

Cork, Richard, 'Figures add up to newfound freedom', The Times, UK, 12 Sep, 1995

Dannatt, Adrian, 'The Luxury of Doing Nothing', Flash Art International, no.183, Summer, 1995

Muir, Gregor, 'Vague', Art & Text, no.51, May 1995

Wakefield, Neville, 'Gary Hume', Artforum, vol.33, no.5, Jan, 1995

Coelewij, Leontine, Martijn van Nieuwenhuyzen (eds.), 'Wild Walls', Stedelijk Museum, Amsterdam, 1995

Freedman, Carl, 'Minky Manky', South London Gallery, London, 1995

Kent, Sarah, 'Shark Infested Waters: The Saatchi Collection of British Art in the 90s', Zwemmer, London, 1994

Searle, Adrian, 'Unbound: Possibilities in Painting', Hayward Gallery, London, 1994

Loock, Ulrich, Gregor Muir, 'Gary Hume Paintings', ICA, London / Kunsthalle Bern, Germany, 1995

Smith, Roberta, 'Gary Hume', The New York Times, 21 Oct, 1994

Searle, Adrian, 'Shut That Door', frieze, no.11, Summer, 1993

Bonami, Francesco, 'Gary Hume at Matthew Marks', The New Yorker, 2 Mar, 1992

Gillick, Liam, Andrew Renton (eds.), 'Technique Anglaise: Current Trends in British Art', London, 1991

Jeffrey, Ian, 'Freeze', 1988